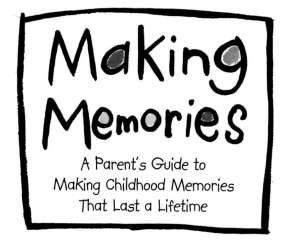

Making Memories

A Parent's Guide to
Making Childhood Memories
That Last a Lifetime

Compiled by Josie Bissett

Illustrated by Debbie Tomassi
Edited by Dan Zadra
Designed by Kobi Yamada & Steve Potter

COM·PEN´·DI·UM™
Publishing

In Loving Memory of Larry Estes

whose life was lived simply and beautifully.

Your smile will live in our memories forever.

Acknowledgements

To Mom and Dad, I am eternally grateful for your giving me such great memories to look back on, and to pass on to my family. I love you both!
To my publisher, Compendium Inc., it's a breath of fresh air working with a company that is so dedicated to making positive changes in people's lives.
To Kobi Yamada, for your faith and friendship—you are one of a kind!
To my editor, Dan Zadra, thank you for your inspiration and wisdom; without you this book would not be possible. **To Debbie Tomassi and Compendium's design team, Steve Potter, and Jenica Wilkie**, thank you for your fun and creative designs and illustrations. **To my publicist and friend, Nancy Iannios**, please know how much I appreciate all your hard work and truly love working with you.

To Tote Yamada, Connie McMartin, Cristal Spurr, Sherrill Carlson, and Debbie Cottrell, for all the wonderful things you do behind the scenes.

Special thanks to all the parents throughout the world who shared with me your fantastic memory makers. I have implemented many of them in my life and have found great joy!

Dedicated to Rob, Mason and Maya Estes. Cheers to making memories! Oh, how I love you.

Printed in Hong Kong

Make a memory
with your children,
Spend some time to
show you care;
Toys and trinkets
can't replace those
Precious
moments that

you share.

—Elaine Hardt

*If we want to have wonderful
memories for our children, now is the time
to do something wonderful with them.*
—Anne Granier

Dear Parents,

*Every parent wants to do the best possible job raising
their children. We try to provide a safe home, good
food, a great education, strong values, and lots of love.
Of course, one of the most important gifts we can give
our children is great memories. So, why not do it on
purpose instead of leaving it to chance?*

*Oh, how quickly our little ones are gone from our arms.
As the years fly by, and your children grow up to take
their place in the world, there will come a time when
you are no longer with them. But the memories you
create today will accompany them into tomorrow.*

*In good times or bad, great memories will help keep
your children's feet on the ground and their eyes on the
stars. As Isabella Graham once wrote, "Your children's
memories of home and family will one day become
their bridge to the past, their shelter in a storm, and
their wings to the future."*

*I asked myself, "If good memories are so important to
our children, where are the books to guide us in
creating them?" After all, there are literally hundreds*

of wonderful books on childhood nutrition. And yet, good food is eaten and forgotten, while good memories can last a lifetime.

Here, then, is a perfect companion to my first book, "Little Bits of Wisdom." Once again, I turned to everyday parents and grandparents who have walked this path before me—and once again they responded by the hundreds. Thank you, one and all.

So, now it's time to sprinkle fairy dust on the lives of your children. As with "Little Bits of Wisdom," some of the best ideas in these pages are also the simplest. If you're a daddy, put your daughter on your shoulders today and go for a walk. If you're a mommy, grab an apron for your little one today and bake some cookies.

Right now is a good time. Today is the best day to make a memory with your children.

Enjoy!

Josie Bissett

A thousand
dreams dance in
a mother's eyes
as she watches
the crib where
her baby lies.

—Edgar Guest

*Good old days start
with good new days like today.*
—Denise Settle

When my new baby girl, Erica Grace, was born I hung a decorated piece of poster board and a felt tip pen on a string on my hospital door. A note at the top of the board invited friends and family to "Please leave a brief message to welcome Baby Erica." Everyone who came to visit wrote a sweet greeting to our new little one, including the nurses who took care of us!

When we arrived home, we put the message board on the back of our front door, and guests who came to our home also got to write a message to Erica. Oh, and our answering machine was full of messages and well wishes, so I copied every message onto a tape and then burned it onto a computer CD. Years from now Erica will have all the excited voices and written messages from the people who love her most in the world.
—Sarah Campbell Williams

Children love to read with their parents and hear about the day they arrived in the world. While I was recovering from the birth of my son Ben (and had to stay on the couch awhile) I created a "The Day Ben Was Born" book. I used a small photo album that had a space for his picture on the front. I inserted pictures from pre-pregnancy, pregnancy, and birth, alternating with cards that told the story

> *Write your memories in a journal and*
> *you will live life twice.*
> —Alice Paul

of when my husband and I married, then found out we were pregnant, how we told everyone (and their reactions), and our trip to the hospital. I'm sure that as Ben gets older, we will enjoy reading this story over and over again throughout the years.
—Nancy Shapiro

Following in my older and wiser sister's footsteps, my husband and I started writing in a journal the moment we found out I was pregnant. The journals include many love letters to our children and many funny moments and milestones in their lives. We write in the journals every few months and plan to give them to our children when they are older. We feel these "legacy journals" will be wonderful keepsakes for them—a great way to savor our memories and to express to our children our great love for them. A journal is also a great gift idea for expectant parents.
—Natalie Fahrer

During my baby shower for my daughter, my sister gave each guest an index card and asked them to write down a little piece of advice or wisdom on motherhood. All cards were

Our babies are hopes in a blanket.
—Dan Zadra

then placed in separate envelopes and each person put a date on the outside. The envelope could not be opened before that date. Some were to be opened fairly soon, and others were to be opened months or even years later "when the advice would be most needed." It has been a wonderful way to remember that special day, and I look forward to opening the next piece of advice with great anticipation and appreciation. I'm saving each of them so I can give them in a little bundle to my daughter when she grows up and has a daughter or son of her own.
—Stevette Linden

Calligraphy is a tradition in our family. When our daughter, Ashley, was one month old, we cut snippets of her downy hair and made an elegant calligraphy brush with it. It is an artistic souvenir of our little one's first year, and we hope that someday when she too learns to write calligraphy, she can use the brush made from her very first hair to create a special rendering.
—Leo Kok

Everyone generally chooses something special for their baby to wear home from the hospital, but the baby grows so quickly that it isn't worn again. Why

9

*Memories, important yesterdays,
were once todays. Treasure and notice today.*
—Gloria Gaither

not frame it in a shadow box and have a little brass plaque engraved with the birth details and hang it somewhere special. Later, when your children grow up and have kids of their own, you can give it to them to treasure.

—Alex Whitelaw

I have a 2–year-old daughter and a newborn. Some of my favorite memories are of my oldest daughter beginning to talk. The mispronunciation of words is priceless. What better way to reminisce when your children are older than to pull out your "Collection of Priceless Quotes." Just create a colorful notebook to be used whenever your child says something outlandish or mispronounces a word. Write it down in your book and save those memories for years to come.

—Michelle Perkins

I only have
to take up
this or that
to flood my soul
with memories.

—Dorothee DeLuzy

Every loving mother needs to keep a secret place, a place of her own to store her most precious memories so that they may be taken out and looked at whenever and wherever the need arises.

—Mary Miller

For my son, Jeffrey, I bought an ordinary photo box, but instead of filling it with photos, I fill it with memories: His first concert ticket stubs to "The Back Street Boys," his school concert performance schedules; his baby teeth; letters to Santa; a great movie with papa ticket stubs; a few cute notes he left me with the dates and his age; the ticket stubs for a hockey game and a basketball game with dad; camp memories. You see, there are no rules, just a box of memories and a whole lotta love. I also decorated the outside with sparkles, along with his name, birth date, and my most favorite photos. I will give it to him on a special day like graduation from college or maybe his wedding day. It is also a beautiful gift you can start for a friend's child or for your grandchildren.

—Lori Robin Roberts

Here's a great memory that you and a small child can make together as a gift for Mom or Dad on Mother's Day or Father's Day. Change a few words, and it works for grandparents, too. Help the child make one or more handprints on a large

The heart hath its own memory, like the mind.
And in it are enshrined the precious keepsakes,
into which is wrought the giver's loving thought.
—H.W. Longfellow

piece of parchment or a sheet of white poster board. Then, use your felt pen or your computer to compose the following poem below the child's handprint:

Sometimes you get discourage
Because I am so small
And always leaving fingerprints on
furniture and walls.
But every day I'm growing up,
and soon I'll be so tall
that all my little fingerprints will be hard to recall.
So here's a final handprint to remember with a smile
on this Mother's Day (or Father's Day)
when I was just a child.

—Belinda Marritt

I saved my son's, or should I say MY favorite T-shirt from his first year, and put it on his favorite stuffed animal. That way, I can still look at it and remember how cute he was (and how little he was) when it fit him.

—Debbie Brew

Each of my children has a "Happy Box." It's just a plain old shoebox that they've decorated in their own special way. When something makes them very happy, they place an item that reminds them of that moment in the box. Maybe it's a card, or a note, or a picture, or a ribbon that they've won. Then, whenever they feel sad, they can go to their Happy Box and pour through memories of better days. It never fails to brighten their spirits.

—Janine Duncan

When we found out we were expecting our second child, we did everything we could to help prepare our three-year-old, Emily Rose, for the arrival of her baby sister. In preparing the new baby's nursery, I chose a beautiful water color painting that Emily had painted at her pre-school. I printed Emily's name and date in the corner of the painting, just like a real artist would do, and had it professionally matted and framed.

Before her little sister was born, we hung Emily's painting over her crib so it would be there when we brought her home from the hospital. This was Emily's very special contribution to

Now the distance holds us apart,
The boundaries have no end.
I'll hold the memories in my heart.
You're my mother, my best friend.
—Unknown

her new little sister's room. She is so very proud of her piece. She shows it to everyone who comes to visit and absolutely beams with joy as she points it out to guests. I'm sure it will be something Emily's sister will treasure for all time, and it will be a touching heirloom for her to pass down to her children.

—Sarah Campbell Williams

When I was a little girl, my mother and I used to walk into town to go shopping together. We always walked through the courtyard of the church we attended and would stop to pick four-leaf clovers. She had a hill that she used to pick four-leaf clovers from when she was a child, too. She had an old "special" book that she would press her four-leaf clovers in. Like her, I had a "special" book that I used for my four-leaf clovers. Now that I have three children and two stepchildren I have passed this tradition on to them. We press anything from four-leaf clovers, to fall leaves, to (recently) flowers from our Aunt's funeral. It has always been a sentimental and beautiful way to preserve "little moments" from our past.

—Elizabeth P. Wood

We were stuck in the house for a couple of days due to a snow storm—so, I thought of a fun project to do. We painted our two children's hands all different colors and let them make handprints on their "own" wall in a hallway. We now frame their drawings and hang them on that same wall. It's been two years and already it's so much fun for them to put their hands against the prints and see how much they have grown, as well as to see their masterpieces displayed on "their" wall. The only problem is: How will I ever be able to bring myself to repaint these precious walls?

—Diane Tridente

I have started a charm bracelet for my 2-year-old daughter. I encourage family members and friends to give her charms that represent themselves in some way. For example, I hate to cook, so I am going to give her a frying pan charm. My mother loves to garden, so she will give her a flowerpot charm. I bought the charm bracelet at James Avery, and they have every charm imaginable. Also, I will give her charms on special occa-

sions and holidays. At Easter, I gave her an Easter
bunny. Next year, I might give her an egg charm.
The neat thing is, I am writing down who gave her
each charm so this can be a memory of all of the
special people in her life.

—Kristi Skeen

When I was a child, my mom and dad were
fixing a small section of our front cement sidewalk.
They had each of us four kids put our handprints in
the cement and used a stick to write our name
under the handprint. My mother has lived in the
same house we grew up in for over 30 years now.
Every time we are by the sidewalk we stop to
compare our "grown up" handprint to what it was
as a child. I have continued the tradition with my
daughter. This summer we used a stepping
stone kit (sold at craft stores) to make an
impression of her hands. Even if we move
to a different home, we will always be
able to take it with us. I am sure she
will enjoy comparing her hands as
she grows up, just like me and
my Mom.

—Meg Fouts

*It isn't the big pleasures that count the most;
it's making a great deal out of the little ones.*
—Jean Webster

I believe that memories are priceless, and my business is based on this belief. My friend and I started a company that takes other people's stacks of disorganized photos and childhood memorabilia and we arrange them into albums for them to treasure. One of the best tips I have is to make an ABC book for your kids using the ABC's of their life. For example, on the "M" page, there might be a picture of Mom, or the time you visited Montana, etc. It's a great way for the young ones to learn their ABC's, too, by immersing them in beautiful memories.

—Jennifer Whitten

I keep a scrapbook for each child to put their artwork in. I don't keep every single piece (that would be impossible), but the special ones, the really cute ones, go into their scrapbook. I date each piece, and every once in awhile we bring out some of their old scrapbooks and laugh at the wonderful, silly, funny things they drew.

—Kandice Brackenbury

Dreams come
a size too big
so that we can
grow into them.

—Josie Bissett

We do not remember days,
we remember moments.
—Cesare Pavese

My daughter is 8 months old. Every month on the 21st (the day she was born), I weigh her, measure her, and take a picture of her with the same teddy bear she was given as a baby present. Someday she will be able to look back at those pictures and watch herself grow, month by month, until—at last!—she is bigger than the teddy bear.
—Lynda Aerts

We live in Texas and every spring it is a common sight to see fields of bluebonnets (our state flower) growing everywhere. They are truly breathtaking. My husband and I take our son to the same field every year and take his picture. We make a day of it and get our son dressed up, usually in his Easter outfit, and take a picnic lunch with us. So far we have three photos of him to enjoy. As a family we like to talk about the days, remembering what we saw and discuss in the photos how the field has grown each year and how he has grown too. My hope is that we continue to take these photos and he will have a photo album of bluebonnet memories to share with his own children.
—Gretchen Champion

Each year at the Holidays, I take a picture of my son seated in my rocking chair. It's fun to see how he's grown and how his feet now dangle over the edge. Soon our holiday pictures will feature his baby brother, and I know the tradition will continue so long as they both fit in the seat!

—Melissa Wilson

Every year on each of my children's birthdays, I take a photo of them standing at our front door. Over the years we see their growth and development (and the changes in our door!), exactly one year apart. I also weigh and measure them on that day, just as I did when they were babies. And, because I believe birthdays are all about making you feel special, I paint a birthday plate and mug at a pottery place. These are used by each member of our family on their birthday—and then put away and saved.

—Lori Bodin

I have always made homemade Christmas ornaments with my two daughters every year. I now have a grandson, and the first Christmas he was

Of all the gifts she gave us, please—
the greatest of these were the memories.
—Isabella Graham

born I decided to do something different. I simply traced his hand onto a brown paper bag and cut out an ornament the size and shape of his hand. Then we stuffed and decorated it, and attached a string for hanging. I also wrote his name, year, and age on the back. He is 4 now and we have a set of four wonderful ornaments to look back on. He now makes them for his parents.
—Tina Robertson

Every Mother's Day, I have a snapshot taken of me with my children. I then put it in a large multi-picture frame that holds all the pictures taken from past years. There, in one special place, is the visual story of how our family and love have grown year after year.
—Ellen Smith

I am the mother of a 5-month-old son and I am planning to do this for my husband for Father's Day. Take a picture of your kids holding a sign saying "Happy Father's Day." Take that same picture with the same sign every year and put them in a photo album just for your husband. Won't it be fun to look back over the years and see how much they have changed!
—Michele Magowan

> Delight in the little things.
> —Rudyard Kipling

My memory maker is a growth board. It is a brightly colored wood board about 5 feet tall and a foot wide, with a measuring stick attached to it. The stick is white, and the board matches the colors in my son's room. About every six months we mark his height and weight on the board next to the yardstick. I started this right after leaving the hospital when he was born. At that time, we dipped his little hands and feet in white-wash, made his prints on the board, and took a picture of him and the board. One day when he is wearing a size 12 shoe, he can look back and see how tiny his hands and feet once were, and what he looked like the day he made them.

—Elena Reduzzi

I have a dress that I wore as a little girl. That dress was also worn by my daughter and is now packed away waiting for her future daughter. I have a picture of me in that dress, and a picture of my daughter in the same dress. They are side-by-side in the same frame, and it means the world to both my daughter and me.

—Melissa Robinson

You never know when you're making a memory.
—Rickie Lee Jones

I love dressing my children; the clothes are adorable and hold so many memories. I can't save all the outfits so I save only the ones from special portrait days—like their one-year portraits and their birthday party outfits. When they grow up, they will have the special photos as well as the actual outfits they wore, and perhaps this will conjure up fond memories of special days gone by.
—Brooke Green

I took all my son's receiving blankets—nine of them—and had them made into a precious quilt! I love it, it's soft, and it will be something he'll have for his own children later in life.
—Babystyle

I am saving special clothes that my sons wore throughout the years, including pieces from flannel shirts, first bathing suits, holiday costumes, sports uniforms, etc. When they grow up and marry, I will sew the pieces into patchwork quilts for their children.
—Sarah Engelmann

My mother gave my newborn daughter a christening hat made from a lace handkerchief. Years later, on my daughter's wedding day, the stitches

Memories will bring you love from the past, courage in the present, hope for the future.
—Sascha

were removed and she used it for "something old." A wonderful, treasured memory.
—Babystyle

When I was pregnant, my mother had my wedding dress made into a christening dress for my child. It was basically a miniaturized version of my wedding dress, with the back beading made to look like the train. Our second child also wore this dress at Christening. My hopes are that when my children have children they, too, will wear this. It is special because it was worn the day my husband and I started our life and family together.
—Lisa Seymour

Each year on my children's birthdays I write them a letter, reviewing all their achievements and adventures for that year, including funny sayings, favorites, dislikes, milestones etc. I plan to present each of them with a bundle of letters on their 21st birthday. It will be a little like a mini life story. Not only does it document their joys and sorrows, it helps me remember how I felt, how much I love them and how precious they are to me. And they will be able to see how much we loved them every year of their lives.
—Patti Freeman

I can still remember
rocking them to sleep
in the middle of the
night, to soothe them
back to sleep after a
stomachache or bad
dream, the songs I
would make up.

—Betty Friedan

My heart is filled with love and care that grew from seeds you planted there.
—Debbie Tomassi

Every night, after I finish reading my 6-year-old daughter a story, we look out her window for her magic unicorn. This is a wonderful flying golden unicorn that takes her and me to somewhere magical in our dreams. Before she falls asleep, we decide which cloud we want to visit in our sleep together—a park cloud, a carnival cloud, a book cloud or a zoo cloud—anything we can dream up. We have been doing this every night for four years, and my daughter always falls asleep with a happy dream and her mommy by her side.
—Anne Leedom

A great way to give your child good memories is to sit down at bedtime and make a journal entry with him or her. They'll tell you what they want to write and you just copy it down. Or you can stimulate their imagination by asking them to tell you what they want to be when they grow up, what they would do with a million dollars, who they admire most in the world, etc. It's fun, brings you closer, and records a new memory every day.
—Suzanne Spiteri

When I was a child I hated bedtime because I was scared. One of my fondest memories is a game my mother would play with me called,

When things got scary, I could always run to Mom and Dad. Years later I still can.
—Cat Lane

"Close your eyes and not a peep, who will watch over me while I sleep?" I would close my eyes and she would choose a doll from my collection and give it to me. With my eyes still closed, I would hold it and try to guess which doll it was. Then that would be the doll I would sleep with that night. It made bedtime fun, brought my mother and me closer, and also made me feel safe and secure.
—Meg Fore

My two children are 2 and 3, and I have taught them to take turns tucking each other in at night. They give a kiss, favorite animal (bear for my son and bunny for my daughter) and then pull the covers up. Sometimes it's silly, like when they kiss each other's nose or hand, or sometimes my son will try to put my daughter into her crib. Of course, Mommy and Daddy have to give kisses goodnight after them. It's definitely become a family thing at bedtime; it's very relaxing for everyone, and creates a special memory.
—Alleen Sangiuliano

Each night at bedtime, we discuss with our sons what their favorite part of the day was and then log it into journals. It is fun and interesting to share the happenings of the busy day and see

When you thought I wasn't looking,
I felt you kiss me goodnight, and I felt loved.
—Unknown

the beauty in the smallest things as they do. We also hope that this will encourage them to journal throughout their lives.

—Gina Gould

I am an 8-year-old girl. My mother is a very good one. We decided to send some ideas for your book. My mother sends notes in my lunch box, which I love. We also have something called best and worst part of your day. I have a little brother, so we also have something called family hug. It is when the whole family has a hug before bed. We get along very well.

—Katie

Being a mom is absolutely the best thing in the whole world! When I am tucking my children into bed at night, I tell them to throw their bad dreams at me so I can take them away. Then I throw "good" dreams and memories to them (such as going to Nana's cottage, swim-ming in the lake,

29

No day ends if it makes a memory.
—Jackie Erickson

spending time with their cousins, playing at the park, visiting the farm, etc.). From there, they can go right to sleep with pleasant, fun pictures dancing in their heads.

—Kandice Brackenbury

We all sing lullabies to our children before bedtime, but my 3-year-old son, Ryan, has decided to change tradition by singing "Nite Nite" songs to me. My husband works evenings, and Ryan usually falls asleep with Mom before Dad gets home. He first started singing Barney's, "I love you, you love me, we're a happy family" as Mom's lullaby from Ryan. He has now graduated to singing "Three Little Monkeys" and then the ABC song. When Grandma came to town, she asked Ryan to sing the ABC song for her, but he looked up innocently and said, "No, I can't. That's my mommy's special 'Nite Nite' song and I only sing it to her before we go to sleep." I'm sure this will remain a memory that he and I will always cherish.

—Angela Reid-Tupper

Life is fun and food,
and love and you,
Kodachromed for
future view.

—Jeri Spelling

Is anyone missing his or her baby pictures? It seems that everyone (myself included) cannot seem to find any baby pictures of themselves to compare with their own babies. My solution? Every time I get pictures developed, I get "triples" instead of doubles. I have three albums—one for me and both of my little ones— that I add pictures to every time I have film developed. In this album I have included pictures  of myself when I was pregnant, and also my sonogram pictures. This way, my twins will never say that they don't have any baby pictures of themselves when they get older! I plan on surprising them with these albums as a keepsake when they have their first child.

—Cary Beth Devine

I buy my children their own disposable cameras for special occasions and let them take their own pictures. This allows them to make their own memories of the event, and I can see the things that they thought were important. Even my 3-year-old has learned to take pretty good snapshots. I put the pictures in their own photo album.

—Ellen Smith

My parents both retired shortly after I was married and moved out of state. When I found out I was pregnant, my parents were upset that they wouldn't be with me. We talked and e-mailed frequently. My mom was present when I gave birth to my daughter. This gave her such joy and happiness, but hurt her so much when she would have to leave and go home. I decided to video my daughter as much as possible every month, record it onto a tape and send it to my parents. Now, my parents get to see my daughter grow and feel like they are a part of her life. We talk after they receive each video, discussing how much my daughter has changed and how fast she is growing. This really makes my parents happy, and they have promised to save each tape as a future gift to their grandchildren in the years to come.

—Penny Sonkin

The little things that make life sweet are worth their weight in gold. They can't be bought at any price, and neither are they sold.

—Estelle Hoover

My memory maker is to capture your little one's voice at every age possible. I started recording my daughter's and son's first words and songs, along with cute things they would say. I eventually put the entire collection on a CD as a gift for their Daddy on Father's Day. On the drive to work, he sometimes pops the CD in and listens to our daughter saying "Hi," and "Dada," or singing "You Are My Sunshine." In no time at all these little voices change, so make your memory now with a CD filled with priceless sounds of your children.

—Sharon Heaps

Moms and dads can both get involved in memory making by making videos and taking pictures. I recommend iMovie by Apple so that you can easily edit each video, e-mail it to other family members, or even put it in on your own family website. It's easy to learn, and the memories are absolutely irreplaceable.

—Lysha Stanford

Our three children are all grown now with children of their own, but when they were little, we would record conversations with them. It might be at bedtime or a special time set aside during the day. One or both of us would record as they would tell

us about their day or sing little songs that they had
learned. Our middle one even snuck back to where
we had left the recorder while we ate dinner and
recorded a special version of Goldilocks and the
Three Bears. We were very surprised the next
time we listened to the tape and realized what the
whispering voice was saying. When they started
having children of their own, we made copies of
the tape which they now share with their children.
Needless to say, they had quite a few laughs, and
we had a few tears mixed in.

—Sandra Maxwell

I made both my children an audio tape of special
songs that I have sung to them since I carried
them—songs about children, love, bedtime, or just
songs that remind me of their spirit. They both love
listening to their tapes and know every song. If we
hear one on the radio, my daughter will say,
"Mommy, it's our song!" I know they will forever
think of me and their childhood whenever they hear
these special songs and know how special they are
to me.

—Diane Tridente

Our three boys have always enjoyed putting
together their own plays for my husband Rick and

me to watch. Fortunately we decided to record
these plays so that we could keep them forever. It
was so heartwarming to watch the boys collabo-
rate together to plan their next script, plus it was a
great way to get their creative minds working.
We captured every play the boys put together
from Christmas to Halloween to just-for-fun plays.
The boys are teen-agers, now, and are no longer
into making plays, so those videos mean the
world to us.

—Stacy Valdez

Many proud parents make it a habit to record
their children's milestones and special occasions
on video. But a great way to observe the development of your child is to use one video tape to
record ONE recurring special occasion, year after
year—their birthday, first day of school, Christmas
morning, etc. For example, we use the same
master tape to record my daughter's birthdays
each year. This makes it easy to watch how she
has changed from a darling, chubby baby to a
smart, funny, beautiful 5-year-old who loves to
sing. She loves watching the changes each year,
and so do we.

—Mona Pilecki

I had pictures taken every few weeks during both my pregnancies, including my growing tummy, the progress on the nursery, and how my daughter was preparing to become a big sister (for my second pregnancy). I then had videos made entitled, "Waiting for Our Baby" with special songs in the background, showing how happy we were to be expecting an angel, how I grew and, most important, how much we loved our babies even before they arrived. My children, now 5 and 2, watch their videos over and over with huge smiles, calling them their special videos. They just love seeing how they grew in my tummy and how special they were to us from the very first second.

—Diane Tridente

Each year around Thanksgiving, I take pictures of extended family members (cousins, aunts, uncles, and both sets of grandparents) and then group them into months according to their birthdays. Then I create a birthday photo calendar for the coming year. My children look forward to seeing whose birthday is coming up and it also helps them to have a little patience when waiting for their own birthday.

—Patricia Notholt

When I was with my father,
when I was just a child,
the world was filled with
wonder and every place
was wild. And every day
was magic, and Santa Claus
was true, and all the things
that mattered were
things my father knew.

—Marsha Jeffrey Hendrickson

*The night you were born, I ceased being my
father's boy and became my son's father.
That night I began a new life.*

—Henry Felsen

Laughter shared with your children is a gift they'll
always cherish. My husband regularly sits down
with our 4-year-old daughter to watch cartoons
together. You can hear them giggling and belly-
laughing from every room in our house. She
recently informed us that she could not laugh at
cartoons if her father was not there. "It's not the
same without Daddy." Silly, sure. But I know their
special "laugh time" will be a sweet memory to her
because my husband has wonderful memories of
the exact same time spent with his parents.

—Shelley Yeatts

My husband and I both work full-time jobs. The
time we have with our two boys is precious and we
try to make it as special as possible for them. Each
evening after work is "family" time. We don't take
phone calls or run errands—we stay at home five
evenings a week and concentrate solely on the
boys. We take walks, play in the backyard, read
books, or play hide 'n seek. Then, to wind the
evening down, we load the tub with plenty of
bubbles and lots of toys—all four of us packed in
one tiny bathroom. There is nothing more precious
to your children than the gift of time! They don't
care how you spend the time, just as long as you
make them feel like they are Priority One.

—Karen Passmore

The work will wait while you show the child
the rainbow, but the rainbow won't wait
while you finish the work.
—Pat Clifford

My husband, Erik, is a loving father who feels that tradition and the little things are the most important memories. He includes our daughter in every little detail of holiday fun—carving pumpkins, hanging Christmas lights and ornaments, making homemade pumpkin pies at Thanksgiving. It's Erik who takes her to her craft class and is at times the only father at our Gymboree class singing and dancing around. I love his spirit and so does she.
—Sylvia V. Patten

I was definitely "Daddy's little girl." Every year, at every holiday, Dad would go out and select one of those festive holiday pins for me—a different one each time. He would always pin it on me in the morning before Mom woke up, so it was our special time. I would wear it all day, and then he would help me pin it to a card so I could show it off at school before storing it away with the others. I collected many of these pins over the years, and while most of them are made of plastic, they are priceless to me.
—Sandra Jones

When I was 10, my father got a harebrained idea and decided to build the biggest snowman in our neighborhood. By Sunday night it had turned into

You will pass this way only once. Do it right.
—Rob Estes

the biggest snowman in the city. The local TV stations came out and did a story that appeared on the Monday night news, after which people from all over the city drove by our home in awe. I remember that Dad built the two huge legs by dragging galvanized garbage cans packed with snow and dumping them, over and over, one on top of the other. By the time he was finished (and exhausted), our snowman's head was all the way up to my bedroom window on the second floor, and Dad inserted the eyes (two huge potatoes) by standing on a ladder. It took weeks for it to melt. For the next several years (whenever snowfall allowed) this remained a tradition in our family. By the time I went off to the Army, Dad's annual "snow giant" had inspired imitators all over the city—a great memory.

—John Makowski

> It doesn't matter who my father was;
> it matters who I remember he was.
> —Anne Sexton

As a little girl, my Dad was dedicated to making my life magical. He had a fun way to encourage me to read. The "Book Fairy" would often leave a new book under my pillow, and my Dad and I would spend time reading the book together. I was well on my way by the time I was 4! Dad, who traveled a lot on business, kept close with me by sending letters to me when he was away or even just at the office. Even though we all lived in the same house it was very exciting for me to receive these letters, and I felt so important to be getting mail like a "grown-up."

—Erin O'Sullivan-Smith

My dad would periodically "feel the breeze" with my sister and me at night before bed, especially in the summer months. It was dark and we would have all the lights out, and then we would all peek out the window, feeling the fresh air on our faces. We would watch for lights in the other houses and imagine what that family might be doing while whispering to each other the whole time. Or we would just smell the night air and watch the stars. It was a sweet time with Dad, and we often asked Daddy to feel the breeze with us. It is a memory I will always cherish. I have started to "feel the breeze" with my son and, although we live in the

That best portion of a good man's life,
His little, nameless, unremembered acts
of kindness and of love.
—William Wordsworth

country and don't have many house lights to watch, we enjoy the fresh air, seeing the leaves move, watching for animals, or just looking at the moon and having a quiet time together.

—Amy Mason

One of the hardest times in my life was when I was eight and my parents got divorced. They spent most of their time trying to make ends meet so that my brother and I could still lead comfortable lives. Any spare time that my dad had was devoted to being with us. One of the most resourceful ways we made time for each other is that in the summer, I would meet my dad at the ferry after work. From there we would walk all the way home and, along the way we would always pick bundles of wild flowers to brighten our house.

Now I'm 16 and have my driver's license. When I drive to school, I drive on the same road my dad and I picked wildflowers on. I can still picture my dad walking along the side of the road with me on his shoulders holding a giant bouquet of flowers, and the two of us chattering away. If you're a daddy, put your daughter up on your shoulders and take her for a walk every chance you get.

—Rose Zadra

In the childhood
memories of every
good cook
there's a large kitchen,
a warm stove,
a simmering pot,
and mom.

—Barbara Costikyan

As I grew up, my mom and I always spent one whole day baking Christmas cookies. It was something I looked forward to every year—just me and my mom in the kitchen all day making all kinds of wonderful treats. Now that I have a baby girl of my own I plan to carry on the same tradition. In fact this year, when she was only 6 months old, we made batches of those special cookies with her in her high chair in the kitchen and Christmas music playing in the background.

—Terri Emmett

I feel that memories grow out of consistency. My mother has never changed our holiday meals; the recipes and ingredients always stay the same. Her five children look forward to the turkey stuffing being the same. Every year the same tin is filled with delicious Christmas cookies. We fight over a piece of special coffee cake at Easter. This has also instilled the desire to know each recipe so that we can share them with our children when Mom is gone. I have begun a recipe book for my family, broken down by holiday. If you're craving pinwheel cookies, you can find them in the book under "Christmas" because that's their special time. Included in the cookbook are memories, such as the time Dad snuck in and put too much pepper in the soup for New Year's Day. We have fond memories of each holiday, because we know that my mother and father worked hard to keep them the same.

—Gretchen Champion

Good cook! That's what my dad and granddad would yell out (loud enough for the entire neighborhood to hear) whenever my mom or grandmom would lay a feast on our table. Today, everyone in my family, including our three kids, takes turns making dinner. We've been doing this since the kids were old enough to lend a hand, and now they each have their own specialties and can prepare them with little or no help. Part of the tradition is to personally thank the person or people who prepared the meal, by calling out "Good cook, Janie!" or "Good cook, Dad!" at the end of the meal. I know it's not a big thing, but it's a piece of family praise that has survived four generations.

—Jim Pedica

*Of course, the most indispensable
ingredient of all good home cooking is love
for those you are cooking for.*
—Sophia Loren

Every Sunday morning we make pancakes—not just regular old buttermilk pancakes, but ones that are colored with food coloring and made into shapes. It started with my husband making the pancakes alone, but now the kids (boys, 2 and 4) help mix everything together, choose the colors, and the shapes. We've made rainbows, hearts for Valentine's Day, cars, trains, houses, bunnies, our names, letters, and numbers. The shapes are done freestyle, so they don't always look like what they are supposed to be, but the kids appreciate them anyway. We hope one day, when we're old and gray, the kids will do the whole thing for us!

—Michelle Ramirez

Most of my relatives live in Canada, and we live in California. I really miss the big family gatherings. I especially miss the tasty cranberry sauce Aunt Cindy made every Thanksgiving. So I decided to talk to all my relatives and compile a Family Recipe Book. Some of my relatives even located recipes from my great-great-grandmother. I input all the recipes on my computer and had the finished book profession- ally bound. We now have a fantastic recipe book that I can pass on to my children. My hope is that the book will continue to be passed down and added to for many generations to come.

—Lisa Steele

Traditions and routines are so comforting to young children. In our family we sit down for family dinner every single night, with no TV, phones, or other distractions. We automatically sit in the same seats at the table. Even when we go to restaurants, we sit in the same configuration. After a busy day of being a toddler or pre-schooler, our kids (ages 4, 3, and 4 months) know they have their own valued place at the table and in the family.

—Meaghen Hoang

Help your children celebrate their heritage— and create great memories in the bargain—by teaching them to make and package their own ethnic foods with family "brands." If you combine both sides of our family, we are a weird mixture of Italian, Polish, and Jewish. Each year our teen-agers take to the kitchen to make their own Italian biscotti, salami and wine vinegar (the recipes, spices, and ingredients are all simple and readily available). They also make yummie Polish sausage and jars of sauerkraut. And last year they made fairly decent Kosher pickles for the first time.

By tinkering with stock recipes, the kids quickly develop "secret family recipes" that are a source of pride. To complete the memory, our children create artistic homemade labels on our PC and give their "branded" creations away at Christmas and Hanukkah. Of course, "Pastorini's World-famous Polish Sausage", or "Pastorini's Quintessential Kosher Pickles" may sound a little confusing— but it definitely reflects our family's mixed heritage, and we are having a ball with our little product lines.

—George Pastorini

I live in a very hot part of Australia. When I was a little girl, I have great memories of sitting on the trampoline under a sprinkler, eating ice cold watermelon! We have passed this tradition on to my 2-year-old daughter, Lily. Now she sees the watermelon come out of the fridge and races to the trampoline! We have adorable photos of her blissfully spitting water-melon seeds and beating the heat.

—Angie D'Arcy

There are perhaps no
days of our childhood
we lived so fully as
those we spent with
our parents in play.

—Dale Thomas

I still get wildly enthusiastic about little things. I play with leaves. I skip down the street and run against the wind.
—Leo Buscaglia

My best memory maker is really quite simple: Let your children jump in rain puddles. My son, Rob, knows that if there is a puddle, he can jump in it. I give him a minute or two of all-out splashing and he thinks he is king of the world. I'm sure he will teach his one-year-old sister, Darcy, to do a dance in them, too. Shoes and socks and feet eventually dry—but his laughter is something that will stay with both of us forever.

—Lisa Mergens

Do you remember playing hide 'n seek, or kick the can when you were little? My husband and I like to keep our four boys close to home, so we usually arrange for their friends to come to our house. Like hide 'n seek, one of their all-time favorite games is flashlight tag. Wait until it gets good and dark. Designate a basketball pole or mailbox as the free spot. Whoever has the flashlight is "it." All the others sneak around in the dark and try to make it to the free spot without getting hit by the flashlight beam. You should see the looks on our neighbors' faces as the kids kindly tell them what we are doing and ask them to please turn off their porch lights.

—Donna Stirzel

Take time every day to do something ridiculous.
—Philipa Walker

Have regular "Date Nights" with your child. Make the date well in advance, so you will have something to look forward to (anticipation is half the fun!). Go to McDonald's and actually play in the playground with them, take them to see a movie they want to see, go to the railroad tracks and wave to the people on the trains, or simply take them to the park to swing on the swings or slide down the slide. Let it be their idea, but of course you can always make suggestions. When you're on the date, make them feel as though it's the best day you've ever had and make sure you participate wholeheartedly. It makes them feel as though you two are on the same level for that special time. Always tell them you love them, and end the night with lots of loving hugs and kisses.

—Tammy L. Collins

For my daughter's third birthday, I'm going to rent a costume and go to her day-care center unannounced. I can't wait to see the look on her face when "Winnie the Pooh" or "Bob the Builder" walks in and makes her day special. When she

has children of her own, she'll still be telling the story of when Grandma came to school and made a fool of herself. I want my child to have fun memories of us, always laughing, especially at ourselves.

—Joann Bluett

My husband is a fire fighter. One night each week he is on his 24-hour shift, and my daughter Samantha and I are alone—just the two of us doing something special. Whether it's renting a fun movie, getting a Happy Meal, or staying up a little later than Daddy might allow, it's just "us time." Whenever my father was away my Mom and I used to do that same thing, and it remains one of my most treasured memories of childhood.

—Sylvia V. Patten

My parents have a special night with my brother called "Big Bed Night." On this special night, my parents and brother rent movies and watch them, while eating popcorn of course, in my parents' big bed. I do not participate because I am 29 years old—too big for even the big bed. My brother is 11. He was adopted when I was 18, and I cannot imagine life without him or my parents.

—Christy Jones

There is something in every season, in every day, to celebrate with thanksgiving.
—Gloria Gaither

I have three beautiful girls ages 1, 9 and 12. For the past few years I have continued a ritual with my two eldest daughters. Every other week, usually on a Friday evening, we have a Girl Party! Daddy's not allowed to join in. We make a big bowl of popcorn, sit on the living room floor with pillows and sleeping bags and watch a movie, talk, and laugh. I also do the girls' toenails and fingernails, including soaking, filing, buffing, polishing—the works! They love having Girl Parties; memories are made of this!

—Tracy Calver

Sing and dance with your children every day. Not only is it fun to act silly and dance around, but it is good exercise. I have a few lively CDs, and the minute I put one on, my daughter knows we are going to get goofy, have fun, and make memories!

—Heather Stenz

Summers and weekends can get boring sometimes. My mom (mother of six) made a little recipe card box full of fun things to do. Most were simple activities that she collected along the way, or snipped out of magazines. For example, make a zoo with stuffed animals and blocks; play with play dough; pretend you are in a circus; make a collage using old magazines, etc. Part of the magic was the box itself, and the fun of poring through it for the one idea that struck a child's fancy that day. Today, I am a 25-year-old college student and nanny, and I use my mom's recipe card box with the children I watch. They love it, and I hope to some-day have children of my own who love it too.

—Mary Belton

I have started having popcorn parties at night. We take a blanket out on the lawn, and each person gets his or her own popcorn bowl. We watch the stars and the airplanes flying right over our house getting ready to land. We also get a flashlight and make shadow images on the fence, and we all have to guess. Sometimes the kids run around while we jiggle the flashlight and it looks like a strobe light. Simple, fun, precious—unforgettable.

—Emily Oldroyd

I am a working mom with my own business. I have so little time to spend with my 2-year-old daughter, not to mention time to clean the house, make the dinner, and wash the clothes. But I am learning how to turn housework into play time and memory time. For example, my daughter loves the story of Cinderella. Every night we get out of our

Don't worry if you have a voice like a band saw—
sing anyway! Your children will melt
to your sound and love you for it.

—Dr. Kendall Franklin

"day" clothes and put on a dress (we call it a gown). We listen to classical music and dance around the house while cleaning. She loves it; she laughs, sings, dances, and even cleans, just like Cinderella! Not only does the house get picked up, but it also tires us both out. We end up going to bed early so we can do it again the next day. I don't know what I would do without my little Cinderella!

—Keri Cooper

At least once a week, usually after dinner, we have sing-a-long. Sometimes we sing a new song they've learned in pre-school, or sometimes it's an old favorite. It's like a mini variety show and always entertaining. Sometimes even Dad gets up and does his rendition of James Taylor!

—Leslie Gregg

Never postpone joy.
—H. Jackson Brown

Each of my kids has her own song that I made up. My girls, Kacey and Kelly, had songs that helped them learn to spell their names. Kelly's is K-E-double L-Y, sung to the tune of "Harrigan." They both knew how to spell their names at a very early age, and those songs are now an important part of our family memory pool.

—Vicki Bluhm

Children love to sing, play instruments, and dance. This memory-making activity will bring your family closer and instill an innate love of music. After a day of play, travel or exploration, ask your children what they learned or what they enjoyed. Help them create rhyming sentences for lyrics. You can put the lyrics to a tune children already know, or create a new one with them. Give the song a title. Add dance steps or moves that help your children remember the words. Play simple rhythm instruments or clap with the beat. Musical parents and older siblings may add piano or other instruments to the song. Perform it for family, friends and in your child's classroom. Keep the words in your child's scrapbook or baby book. Record it on tape and video. As you compile songs over the years, you will create a beautiful medley that encapsulates every stage of childhood.

—Jennifer Tan

> My mother never forgot
> what it was like to be a child.
> —Randall Jarrell

Always be willing to act the age of your child! My 5-year-old was playing in the bath one evening and started splashing me. My first instinct was to put a stop to it, but I knew he just wanted to play with me. Instead of scolding him, I jumped right into the tub, clothes and all, and we had the biggest splash fest we'd ever had. Just hearing his shouts of glee at Mommy in the tub with her clothes on made me realize I had just made a very happy memory for my precious boy.

— Lisette Davidson

Here's a simple thing that every mom can do, and no child will ever forget. Resist the temptation to simply plop your child in front of the TV so you can clean the house in peace. When the TV is on and my daughter is watching Sesame Street or any other program she enjoys, I sit on the floor or couch with her, and we sing the songs, or count, or dance together. I think this will help form memories of how much fun her mom was. And it also helps me remember how much fun it is to be a kid.

— Jessica Krajnalic

Vacations are
a little like love:
anticipated with
relish, experienced
with inconvenience,
and remembered
with absolute joy.

—Kim Keller

*Because of our routines we forget that
life is an ongoing adventure.*
—Maya Angelou

I have three sisters and a brother. We are all grown up with kids of our own now, but we all agree that our parents had a special knack for making memories. As a family we always did what my father and mother called "crack of dawn stuff." If we went trout fishing, we were always in the boat and on the lake at the crack of dawn. If we were driving to California, or to a ski resort, or even to a simple weekend picnic, we had to be in the car and on the road at the crack of dawn. Over the years, I have joined my parents on the edge of a volcano in Hawaii, in a kayak on a game preserve in Alaska, on a stormy ocean beach in Oregon, in a remote duck blind in Montana, and in a Native American cave dwelling in New Mexico—all at the crack of dawn. There's something special and mysterious about rising early as a family and starting your adventure together with the rising sun. Loading the car quietly, we always whispered so we wouldn't wake the neighbors, knowing that we were setting off with the wind and the stars, while they were still snoring away in their boring beds!

—Kelly O'Brien

When we have weekend outings or go away on family holidays we always take along empty scrapbooks and colored pencils for our kids. At the end of the day we encourage them to draw pictures of their favorite sight or memory from that day. These drawings by our children are far more meaningful than most of the pictures we take along the way. We

have made several lovely books that chronicle our vacations as a family, all through the little eyes and hearts of our children and their art.

—Tracie Barwick

When my daughter, Jessica, turned 10, my husband and I arranged a joy flight on a small plane around Brisbane. She always wanted to go on a plane because her older brother had already been on one. From the start of her special 10th birthday until the end we took photos. And Jessica even took the camera with her on the plane. When I got the film developed, I made a collage of all the wonderful pictures and framed it. It hangs in her bedroom, and every time we look at it we smile because of the lovely memories it brings us all.

—Sylvia Perrett

*'Twas her thinking of others made
you think of her.*
—Elizabeth Barrett Browning

When we would go on vacation, my mom would make each of us a portable desk using a 13x9 cake pan with a slide cover, and we would write on top and slide the cover open for our desk supplies. We loved it! She would also wrap up gifts and give us one every time we entered a new state. What fun!
— Ann Riedel

As a stepmother, I worked hard to create little family traditions that would bring us all closer together and create good memories. I remember when we went on our first camping trip together. We built a big fire at night and I asked the boys if they wanted to hear a story that was told to me when I was their age. I put the flashlight under my face and told the story of the Slish-Slosh man. The boys listened eagerly with fear in their eyes. It had been a long time since I had told a ghost story, and I couldn't even remember how it ended—but that's not important. I just let out a loud scream to end the story. The boys jumped and so did my husband, and then we all had a great laugh.
The boys asked if they could tell a story, too, so we passed around the flashlight to each person. It was fun to watch them make up their story as they told it. After each story, we could reward ourselves with lots of yummy smores! We try to take the

boys camping each summer, and they always ask
for the Slish-Slosh story. You see? Even a story
without a proper ending will create a wonderful
memory around the campfire.

—Stacy Valdez

I am 29, but my mom still makes a special effort
to make memories with me. We try to have a
mother-daughter trip each year to a new city. This
allows us to go shopping, to the spa, out to
dinner—all the things a girl likes! If we can't get
away for a few days, we will still have our time and
do those same things right at home. Making
memories is important for kids of all ages!

—Christy Jones

Every few months or so, my husband or I give our
son or daughter a special invitation, placed on their
pillow. We invite them to lunch, shopping expedi-
tions, movies, plays, a walk to the ice cream shop,
an evening of Ping-Pong at home, or whatever.
Just use a plain sheet of paper folded like an
invitation. Write, "You're Invited" in big letters on
the front; put the usual "who, what, when, where,
and why" inside; and insist that the children RSVP,
just like big people do. They love it and never
forget it.

—Susan Mandel

One day at a time—this is enough.
Live in the present and make it so beautiful
that it will be worth remembering.
—Ida Scott Taylor

Our favorite activity is to pack a picnic lunch and go to BWI airport in Maryland. They have an observation area where the kids can play on the playground and watch the airplanes take off and land. It's great fun, exciting for the kids, and some of our best memories have unfolded there.
—Melissa Robinson

For school vacation each year my sons and I plan a special day in our own city. We pretend to be tourists and choose what sights we will see. We visit our favorite toyshop, and they can browse as long as they want! We have ice creams and take a ferry across the harbor. We go to the museum and view the skyline from the top of a high building— all their favorite things. They get to choose, but there's something different every time. The memories we have created are very special—not expensive—and my sons have seen their own town in a way few people ever will.
—Lee Klaverstyn

Long before
I was a success,
my parents made
me feel like I could
be one.

—Toni Morrison

A mother holds her children's hands for a while,
their hearts forever.

—Unknown

Purchase a small
cork bulletin
board, put it in a
prominent place in
your home, and create
a sign for it that says,
"What (your child's name)
Made Today." Then, whenever your
child does that special drawing or painting, proudly display it on the board for all
the world to see. It makes them feel so special
and loved; it also stimulates and reinforces their
creativity.

—Brenda Champion

The one thing I remember growing up that made
a profound memory is that my parents attended
nearly every event (sports, recitals, etc.) which
made me feel very loved. I always counted on
them being there; it means so much. Close your
eyes right now. If you can still see your mom's or
dad's proud face beaming up at you from the
school auditorium, you know exactly what I mean.

—Lisa Summers

From early on, we would throw a mini-party for
any and all school accomplishments. For example,

The sun! The sun! And all we can become!
—Theodore Roethke

participating in a school play or concert, a positive phone call or comment from a teacher, being named captain of a sports team, scoring your first goal or basket, etc. These were all good excuses to call the child down to the kitchen, turn down the lights, yell SURPRISE!—and then have a great dessert. Whatever the occasion, we took every opportunity to make it a celebration.

—Susan Mandel

I try to make the first day of school a positive and memorable start by taking my child into town after school on that first day, having a special meal, and buying a special china ornament to commemorate the occasion.

—Edna Searle

My daughter started school in February this year, so I thought of a great way to maintain our close relationship, have some fun together and build some really beautiful memories. I have arranged for her to take one day off school every term to have a Mommy-Daughter day. It's so special because everyone else is in school, but she and I are playing. We go to the movies, out to lunch, play hopscotch, buy ourselves a treat and really talk. My daughter talks about it for ages afterwards.

—Rebecca Hamblin

In a child's lunchbox, a mother's love.
—Japanese Proverb

Parents or grandparents, if possible try to walk your children or grandchildren home from school now and then. One of my cherished memories is meeting my Italian "Nona" at the school steps each day. She always had a piece of peppermint taffy in her sweater pocket for me. Then we walked the mile or so to my home. In the winter she brought a big red umbrella and I sang, "Rain, Rain, Go Away" for her; in the spring we stopped along the way to pick dandelions or wildflowers for Mom; and in the fall we looked for fallen chestnuts in the leaves, or helicopter seeds from the trees. We didn't talk much, but every word counted on those walks and, oh, the memories.

—Anne Gardelli-Foutz

When I was younger, I loved it when my Mum left me notes in my lunchbox. She would write how lucky she was to have me, how beautiful I was, and that in just a few hours she'd see my wonderful smile again. I'll never forget those notes, I loved them! They made me feel special.

—Chelsea Pimm

About ten years ago, I started writing notes to my three daughters and tucking them in their lunches. What makes it special is our love for the theater

There is so much to teach our children,
and time goes by so fast.
—Erma Bombeck

and movies. I'll write a note and always include at least one movie trivia line or more, and they save the notes. When my girls get home from school or work we go over the notes to see if we guessed our trivia right. It has been really fun. Now that they are older, we do it through e-mail. And guess what? My middle daughter, Jenny, is now a theater major at college!

—Donna M. Arnold

When I fix my daughter her lunch for school, I use a cookie cutter to cut her sandwich into hearts or moons and stars. She says it makes her feel special and happy. The smallest gestures can make the sweetest memories!

—Stacy Ashbrook

As a grade school teacher, I am well aware of the abundance of papers, art projects, and special assignments that go home each and every day. I have a special bin containing only those school papers and projects which my child deems his monthly "best." These are the ones I save. His college graduation party will include a gift containing the full array of his most prized schoolwork throughout the years.

—Toni Kanes

69

One's first book,
kiss, home run
is always the best.

—Clifton Fadiman

*A book is a friendly giant who can steal
your imagination, and take you on a journey
to a joyful celebration.*
—Michael Nolan

This is such a simple idea. Every birthday, I give my children a book. Inside the front cover I write a personal message and the date. Eventually, they will have a collection of books dated throughout their life.

—Kelly Ferguson

My mother gave my sister and me our very own library bags that were our favorite color and had our names embroidered on them. Every other week we took our special bags to the library with Mom and picked out books to read. I remember that bag, the smell of the books I put in it, and the joy of reading them alone or with Dad. "Library Day" with my mom and sister remains a wonderful memory, and I plan on continuing this with my daughter, too.

—Kari Joy Bacon

Now that I am pregnant with my first child, I often wonder what memories will stay with this little one. As a single mom, my mother had to work and do all the chores of home life, but she always made time to be with her two daughters. One of my warmest memories was a morning ritual we practiced. One day a week we would all rise early with the sun, and pack up two bowls

> The Lake is with me today.
> The memory of a feeling.
> And when I feel that thing, I want to paint it.
> —Joan Mitchell

(which my mom had made, since she was a potter), milk and granola. Then we would head to a nearby park and sit on a big rock near the lake. Perched on the rock, my sister and I ate our cereal, the ducks would glide across the pond and the creatures of the park would wake up with us, as my mother read to us. When I think of those mornings I can still see the pond and the sunlight coming through the trees, still hear her voice as she read to us. I am so grateful to my mother for giving us such quality time, love and special memories.

—Laurie Silver

I keep a folder of printed e-mails that my family and I write back and forth about the children. My mom often takes my 20-month-old for an overnight stay and writes me the best e-mails about what they did together that day (to ease my mind when Jake isn't here). She has no idea I'm keeping them, and it makes a great little "e-mail journal" in addition to the regular journals I keep for each of my two children. Sometimes relatives and friends will e-mail a response when I send them a digital

> It's the little things we do and say that mean so
> much as we go on our way.
> —Willa Hoey

photo, and I print out and save the best of those
e-mails, too.

— Margo Rhoades

I recently had to take a 10-day business trip and
leave my 2-year-old at home with her daddy. Since
she's really attached to me, I decided to write her a
short letter for each day I was gone. I dated each
letter so she would read them on the right day. I
also included little presents (stickers, special pen, a
toothbrush with Barbie on it, etc.). My husband put
one in the mailbox each night so she would get her
mail every morning. She just loved it, and in each
letter I would tell her how many days were left
before I got home. It helped me, too; I felt she had
a part of me with her even though I was far away.

—Coralee Collingwood

We like to use color copies of photos to create
our own family stories. For my husband's first
Father's Day, my son, Jacob, and I created a book
based on the Laura Numeroff story, "What Daddies
Do Best." We used the computer to write the
words on each page and then color copied our
favorite photos of Jacob and his daddy. We
mounted the photos on scrapbook paper and glued
them on the pages with the words. I took the book

> What is the little one thinking about? Very
> wonderful things, no doubt! Unwritten history!
> Unfathomed mystery!
> —J.G. Holland

to our local Copy Center and they laminated and spiral bound the book. It is one of our favorite stories to read together. We took this idea and created a story for Jake's cousin, JD, all about cousins, too. The latest book we have created was about Jacob and his visit with his two girl cousins from Texas. They will be moving overseas for a year with their parents, and we were sure to make a copy of our book for Emma and Anna to take with them on their trip.

—Rebecca Downing

If someone gives your child a book as a gift, ask for a snapshot (or take one) of the person who gave the book. Laminate the photo, punch a hole in it, and string a ribbon through the hole. Now you have a bookmark that will stay with your family's childhood books for many years to come.

—Kelly Hudson-van der Walt

My 6-year-old daughter, Olivia, loves to draw and write stories. I am a freelance writer who works from home, so she often copies me. I decided to embark on a joint project with my daughter and we chose a book to make together. The first topic we chose was entitled, "I Love Baby Animals." My daughter illustrated various animals and lovingly

Memories are our greatest inheritance.
—Peter Hamill

colored each picture. I then scanned the illustrations onto my computer and added titles and text. Afterwards, we printed out several color copies, bound them, autographed them, and gave them out as presents to friends, teachers, and family. My daughter gained such pride and a sense of accomplishment by becoming a "published author." And since the project was ongoing, she appreciated all the extra one-on-one time with her mom. The project allowed me to preserve some of her best illustrations and her love of animals. Afterwards, my 3-year-old son, Jared, started begging me to draw pictures of trucks and "put dem in compuder" so that he too could have a book with mommy. I look forward to my next collaboration with my children.
—Lizabeth A. Finn-Arnold

Years ago, whenever I went away or had an argument with my daughter, I would leave small notes on her pillow or in her lunch box, telling her how much I loved her. She is now 19 and just the other day she showed me some of these notes that she has kept and still finds great happiness in.
—Judi Williams

The rules for parents are but three: love, limit and make good memories.

—Don Ward

*Don't run through life so fast that you forget
where you've been and lose where you're going.*
—Kobi Yamada

It was Sunday evening, my son was watching TV, I was making dinner while talking on the phone, and my husband was checking his e-mail. Suddenly the power went out! We quickly lit candles and sat on the floor together and just talked. I was amazed at how quiet our house became. How peaceful and connected we all felt. Life can get so crazy that we lose sight of what's really important. Now, on Sunday evening, as often as possible, we turn off EVERYTHING, light candles and play games, make forts, or just hang out. That moment when the power went out changed our lives. "Getting stuff done" pales in comparison to the memories we are making as a family.

—Josie Bissett

Every Friday night is "family night" for us. My two brothers and two sisters (along with our twenty children!) go out somewhere for dinner. Our children learn the true meaning of family values. At restaurants we use a numbering system to keep track of separate checks, and so the children can sit with each other. I was the third-born, so our tab is always for Family #3. Our children are now entering their teens. It's awesome that they still reserve Fridays for their family!

—Marianne McCoy

I was almost a teen-ager before I realized that my family had been living near the poverty level for all those years. Credit my father's spirit and imagination for making us feel so plentiful. He couldn't take us to Disneyland once a year, but he took us to Home Shows, Car Shows, Boat Shows, and Sport Shows all year long. He would hunt for a cheap family discount ticket, give us each a big plastic bag at the door, and then send us off to the booths, collecting free balloons, plastic pens, and little bags of peat moss. It was great fun to compare our "booty" at the end of the day. No, we didn't get to go to many movies, but Dad did take us (and a big bag of peanut butter sandwiches) to every single parade, outdoor concert, even political rallies—anything that was festive and free—and we relished every minute. He's a grandpa now, and he's still at it. One of our kids' favorite things is to go to Costco with Grandpa on Saturday afternoon— and make the rounds of all the free samples.

Time, love, and

We didn't have much, but we sure had plenty.
—Sherry Thomas

memories are Dad's only currency, but I think he's the richest man alive.

—Janet Fielder

Gifts and memories don't always have to be expensive! Our oldest son, Spencer, just made his first Holy Communion. With four small children, it's impossible to hand out hundreds of dollars for each special occasion. When we asked Spencer what he wanted for his gift for communion, he didn't mention anything specific. When his special day at church was over, his friends rushed over and I heard one say, "So Spencer, how much money did you get?" To which he replied, "Well, $200 from Grandma and Grandpa and Grandmom and Pop." His friend shot back, "Well that's nothing, I got $800, and my friend got $2000." Beaming, Spencer quickly replied, "Well, I got the password to my mom and dad's computer, too!" You see, we have come to know that, in this increasingly materialistic world, it's not always money that makes a kid smile. It's time, trust, and respect that works in our family.

—Ceri Renee Galati

Open a savings account for your child, in the child's name, while he or she is still in grade school—but make a big deal out of it! I remember that my mother dressed me up in the most "adult" outfit that I owned and took me out to lunch on the day we opened my savings account. We went to the bank and I was given my own "register" so that I could keep track of all of my deposits (withdrawals were not even considered!), and I felt so mature. I learned how to take care of my own money, which is especially important for a young girl to learn. One of the best things is that my mother made it a day for just the two of us. It didn't seem like a lesson at the time.

—Patricia Ann Dujari

My husband and I want our children to appreciate the true meaning behind Christmas—which is giving, rather than getting. Thus, we started donating money to a worthy cause—food banks, hospitals, a sick child, etc. We put the money in a sealed envelope to be opened last on Christmas. Included in the envelope is a note explaining our "donation for the season" and a newspaper article about the child we're helping, or whatever cause we're supporting. Over the years, these are stored in a

Some of the most important things
in life aren't things.
—Linda Ellerbee

special box so that our children can someday look back and reflect on the importance of giving from the heart.

—Rebecca Carlson

Tell each of your children a different secret—something exciting for the whole family to look forward to. It can be big or small, but it should be exciting. Then tell each child that they must keep their particular secret between you and them, and must not spoil the surprise by telling the other children. This builds a sense of anticipation and excitement throughout the family, makes each of your children feel special, and helps them learn to honor confidences. My children are now 20, 18 and 16, and I'm sure they never once revealed "OUR SECRET."

—Julie Dale

One of the favorite memory makers at our home is called "Angel Deeds." We have a jar filled with little notes, each one listing a nice thing to do for others. I let the children pick one any time they feel sad or need a boost, because one of the best ways to feel better is to help someone else. The angel deeds are simple enough for kids to do ("Tell someone why you like them"), and our children now beg to do more than one at a time.

—Jennifer Whitten

We are Australians who celebrate our country's multiculturalism by hosting a monthly "Cultural Dinner." This is not a project for the faint of heart, but it's educational, fun, and it brings fond memories for your children and a greater appreciation of people from other cultures. My husband and the children help in the preparation, and we are all fascinated with the unusual dishes and ingredients. I usually tie in music (Chinese, Lebanese, Mexican, etc.) and a travel video. For Mexican Seafood night I had the children make a pinata stuffed with lollies. The kids flipped out when I brought home squid (complete with tentacles), green prawns to shell and crumb, and little octopi to serve on top. I'll never forget their faces, with my 7-year-old bravely displaying his octopus while my 6-year-old squealed in excitement and horror!

—Jodie Powderly

My 13-month-old son, Ian, and I love to go for walks. We've done it since he was a couple of months old. Ian loves to touch the leaves on the trees. Now that he's walking, he can touch the whole tree. I want him to be able to embrace and appreciate the value of nature. So when we take walks now, we have to stop and touch every tree and bush along the way. Ian really helps me to see how simple and beautiful life can be. And each walk can become a special memory.

—Jennifer Borde

We collected tadpoles and watched them turn into frogs. We gathered monarch caterpillars and watched them transform into chrysalis and butterflies. We spent summer nights in sleeping bags learning the stars. My son says he is going to do these things with his children. It didn't cost a dime, but we wouldn't trade the memories for a fortune.

—Ms. Sue Grinsted

Fly kites with your kids on a windy day. The new ones are a breeze (excuse the pun) to fly. My children and I have spent some of our best days together, not only making our kites, but competing (highest kite, biggest kite, weirdest kite, etc.). And when you're down on the ground looking up, be sure to tell your kids (as my father and his father often told me and my sister) that "God gave us kites to remind us to 'look up' in our lives."

—Paul Chinn

In the back of our
little house were
those beloved trees
and a garden of
childhood delights.

—Mary Pickford

Remember the garden and dream new dreams.
—Linda Peterson

Plant a garden with your kids and let them choose their favorite fruits, vegetables and flowers. As a little girl I fell in love with sunflowers one year, and my mom let me plant goliath sunflowers along our entire fence line—what a cheery sight. Another year my Dad sent away for Amazon pumpkin seeds, and we had one that reached nearly 200 pounds by Halloween. I also remember planting a "butterfly garden"—I think it was oregano that attracted butterflies by the dozens—and a "pepper garden." It was fun to bring the beautiful red-hot peppers to school for show-and-tell and dare my friends to eat one. My mom had lots of other garden tricks, too—like cutting an apple the wrong way so she could open it up and show me the hidden star inside the apple. She always told me that there was a hidden star inside me, too, but it was up to me bring it out and show it to the world.
—Molly Terrell

Plant a tree, one for each of your children. Teach them to care for the tree, water it, feed it, and maybe even give it

Hold out your hands and feel
the luxury of the sunbeams.
—Helen Keller

a name. The tree will grow as your child grows, and he or she will learn to respect nature and the outdoors. You will share many wonderful memories together. When the tree is large enough, you can climb it, have picnics under its shade, read stories, and hang wind chimes in its branches.

—Michelle Perkins

We always welcomed spring at our house by going on bird-watching excursions. Mom would grab a picnic lunch, a blanket, and her Audubon book, and off we'd go to the park, arboretum, or watershed. Anyone who thinks bird watching is for pansies is really missing out on an exciting and satisfying memory-making event. My brother, Mike, played football for the Purdue Boilermakers, and he kept his "Birds of North America" book in his car all the way through college. Our family memories of spotting rarely seen birds in our own backyard brought our family together in a way that was almost spiritual.

—Jeri Ann Jones

Every summer I have the children paint round stepping stones, and we put them in the flower beds, up against the trees here and there, or actually use them for walkways. The kids love to

These are the days of miracle and wonder.
—Paul Simon

see how their art techniques have changed over the years, and I love seeing my yard come to life with their creations. After painting, just spray a clear varnish on the stones so the paints don't fade.
—Maria Jenkins

My mother taught me this one, and I've done it with my own kids and, now, my grandkids. Buy a simple, inexpensive hummingbird feeder. Your kids will love watching these amazing little birds go about their business. Even more amazing is to teach your children how to get a hummingbird to land, stock-still, on their open hands. It's easy. Just wait a couple of weeks until the humming-birds have made a regular routine of stopping at your feeder each day. Then have your children stand quietly near the feeder with both hands outstretched, and sprinkle a little feed in their upturned palms. Like a miracle, eventually the humming birds will land and feed right in your children's hands. A sweet memory.
—Tula Mannville

Grandpa George and Grandma Lu had the most wonderful tradition called "Our Little Scarecrows." When we were tykes, they had an orchard with lots of fruit trees, and all the grandchildren from both

> Don't cry *because it's over,*
> smile *because* it happened.
> —Melanie Swift

sides of the family would visit in the summer.
When we arrived, we would all clap and clamor to
go out in the orchard to see our scarecrows.
Grandma created the clothes, hair, and burlap faces
so that each one clearly resembled one of us kids.
Grandpa always took time to brag, telling us what a
good job our particular scarecrow was doing of
protecting the fruit. Later on, when
they retired to a little house,
they still carried on the
tradition in their berry patch
and vegetable garden.
Knowing that my little
scarecrow had protected
my grandparents'
berries always
made them taste
even sweeter. Just
after Grandpa
George passed
away, I received a
big box containing
my scarecrow for
that year. He
wanted me to
have it, and I still do.

—Carol Poole

Cherish each and every
birthday with your children,
and keep them in your heart,
for they are gone
before you know it.
The days of finger paints
soon give way to soccer balls,
prom nights and, finally,
graduation gowns.

—Emitt Wholley

Nothing is worth more than this day.
—Goethe

As we all know, birthdays are very special, so in our house the Birthday Girl or Boy gets breakfast in bed (even on a school day)—and they wake up to a room decorated by the "Birthday Fairy" with colorful balloons and streamers.

—Maureen Nicolosi

While planning my son's first birthday party, I began to think about the recollections that I had of my own childhood milestones. I wanted my son to be able to somehow celebrate these memories later on in life when he was old enough to do so. With that in mind, I mailed him a birthday invitation and card to his own first birthday party. When it was delivered to our home (sealed and postmarked with love) I placed it, unopened, in a special keepsake box. I will do this every year, and someday I will present him with the entire Keepsake Box filled with unopened Mommy Mail. That way he can truly enjoy and appreciate the ongoing celebration I have been living since the day he was born.

—Karen Edeson

At birthday parties we always take a group shot of everyone attending our child's party. Then we can send a personalized "thank you" with the group picture on the front of the card to everyone who

gave a gift or made a contribution to our child's special day. Kids love getting mail and are so thrilled to see a picture of themselves. While most children don't save a thank-you card, they do save a card with a photo of themselves. Years from now, when all my child's friends have scattered to other parts of the country, that simple little snapshot will become a super little memory of their early years.
—Rosie Myers

Each year, write the Birthday Child a one-page letter outlining your special memories over the past year. Be sure to include a list of the child's favorite book, song, saying, foods, etc. Ask grandparents, aunts, uncles, godparents, etc. to write a similar one-pager. Laminate the letters for durability and compile them, along with a birthday snapshot each year, into an ongoing book. When your child is old enough, have him/her create a hand-painted cover for the book. Kids love to hear about their special days. This book provides a great way to keep memories handy for times when they ask to hear about when they were "little." It also serves, in its completion, as an awesome keepsake for a child leaving home.

—Wendy M. Duncan

Every birthday write your son/daughter a letter from the heart. Just write down all your feelings and memories from the year just past and then seal the letter in an envelope. I give my daughter a separate card on her birthday, but not the sealed letter. Those I intend to bundle for her 18th birthday (or perhaps when she has a child of her own), so that she can open and read what I was feeling each year as she grew up.

—Kris Stacey

On my son Joseph's first birthday he was given a Birthday Plate that his uncle hand made at the pottery store. It has some of his current favorite things like balloons, a football, and a bear in a football uniform. This plate is for Joseph to use for his birthday cake from now on. It is a very thoughtful and memorable gift since it was hand made by his uncle.

—Robin Coste

Anniversaries are the marks of the years—
Prodding our reveries,
Saying again and again, remember.
—Calvin Miller

We adopted our son, Jacob, in November of 1998 when he was only four days old. We knew that birthdays would be special for him and our family, but we make his "coming home" day and his "legal adoption" day just as important as his birthday. We have a celebration flag that we hang outside our house on all family birthdays and on Jake's Coming Home Day and his Adoption Day. When Jake's Adoption Day comes around each year in January, we have a big family party. We always end the party with a giant cookie celebration back at our house (we save cake celebrations for birthdays). Instead of bringing Jake an Adoption Day gift, we have family members write him a special letter that we can read together and then save in his "box of special things." The letters are personal letters that family members write to Jacob telling him how special he is and how glad they are that he is in our family.

—Rebecca Downing

In our family we always celebrate half-birthdays. Mom makes a small half-cake and half-hamburgers, and we even wear crazy half-hats. Instead of getting presents, the half-birthday person (including Mom and Dad when their half-birthdays roll around) must make or draw a little something for everyone else. It's a big job, but the half-birthday person is always beaming with pride when his or her presents are handed out. The half-birthday has created so many special memories in our home, and it gives the kids something to look forward to between birthdays.

—Donna Ozias

It's that "little extra something" that seems to become a family tradition and a treasured memory. Every birthday my mother of five would put a little extra surprise on our birthday cake. We couldn't wait to get up and see what was on our cake. For example, my favorite animal was a monkey, so each year my mother put a different collectible monkey figurine on my cake. We had a family party before dinner and enjoyed the cake for dessert. But cake is eaten and forgotten—and many years later I still have all my little monkeys from Mom.

—Kari Joy Bacon

Up on the rooftop—
reindeer pause,
Out jumps good
old Santa Claus.
Down through
the chimney
with lots of toys,
All for good little
girls and boys.

—Yule Song

I've started a sweet Christmas tradition with my daughter that my mom did with me when I was little. Every Christmas morning when I was a child, I always woke up with a candy cane in my hand or somewhere in my bed. It was magical; Santa surely must have slipped it into my hand during the night! The tradition has followed me into my marriage. My mom gave my husband a candy cane the first year we were married and told him that he now had to fulfill the family tradition with our children, and he has every year.

—Marcia Tschopp

It was such a big event in our family when our first daughter, Emily Rose, was born. Two weeks before Christmas, we hosted a small family gathering at our home in honor of Baby's First Christmas. In honor of Emily, I created a tiny four-foot Christmas tree, just for her. I decorated it with white lights, pink roses, and teeny baby shoes she had worn throughout the year. Included were her very first pair of tiny satin booties with lace and pink rose trim, her christening shoes, her first patent leather shoes, her first tiny tennis shoes, and more. We took lots of pictures for the future. The whole evening was a joyous event—a once in a lifetime opportunity to celebrate our new baby girl and to create some wonderful memories together.

—Sarah Campbell Williams

Push the Santa story to the max, and your child's Christmas memories will be immortalized in Technicolor! Put out a glass of milk, cookies and chocolate for Santa; put balloons on the handle of the door of the room that the tree is in (so Santa can find it easily in the dark). Put a trail of lollipops leading from your child's door to the tree, so he/she can follow the trail to the presents when they wake up in the morning. Lo and behold, Santa's refreshments are gone (some crumbs left on the plate), but there is a personal note from him, thanking your child for thinking of him on his busy night. (Be sure to save those notes in a box for when your child grows up). And let's not forget to leave a bowl of water and some carrots outside for those

Joys divided are increased.
—Josiah Holland

hard-working reindeer. Of course, the carrots, too, will have bite-size pieces missing from them come morning!

—Sandra Fedele Waller

I am the mother of three beautiful daughters, now 23, 19 and 15. Here is a Christmas memory maker that I started about 15 years ago. We each draw a name and you have to hand-make something that fits the personality of the person you drew. We exchange these hand-made gifts on Christmas Eve right after church. We have come up with some really unique gifts over the years—picture collages, plaques, doll clothes, food treats, a key rack, an Advent doll. One of my favorites is a wooden bank with Aladdin inside that my husband carved for my daughter Tiffany when she was 5. I know my daughters will continue this tradition with their own families. I also started a journal listing all the gifts we have made over the years. Definitely a great memory maker for the family and something I know my daughters will treasure when I'm gone.

—Donna M. Arnold

One Christmas, my daughter received a packet entitled, "Santa's Magical Stardust." It's a simple mixture of oats and gold glitter, accompanied by a little poem. The poem instructs you to sprinkle the Stardust on your lawn on Christmas Eve, and recite the verse. The glitter will sparkle so that Santa can see it from the sky, and the oats will attract the reindeer. My daughter loved it! Every year since, it has become a tradition to make up a batch of "Santa's Magical Stardust." It is great to sprinkle in Christmas cards, but of course we always set some aside for our own family to sprinkle on the lawn on Christmas Eve.

—Kimberley MacDonald

I make Memory Balls for my three children each year just before Christmas. I purchase clear plastic ornament balls (they come in two halves so they can be sealed). I place significant mementos inside: Lost teeth, lock of hair, school photograph, a tiny scroll written with things that were important to them that year, a list of their friends, their dreams, days that were special, moments that were sad, funny, etc. Seal the ball and then decorate with a glitter pen, including the year and name of your child, and attach a Christmas bow. We now have 25 to hang on our tree this Christmas, and every year we hear those words, "Oh, I remember when..." Note: When kids say, "But I

Life is like a puzzle without the picture. You put it
together day by day.
—Miesha Jackson

thought the Tooth Fairy took my teeth"...I just told
mine that I left a note for the Fairy asking if she could
leave one tooth behind for my children's Memory Ball.
The fact that I am on speaking terms with the Tooth
Fairy has impressed my children no end.

—Julie Hoare

Making popcorn balls with Mom and Dad for Santa
instead of cookies—we had such fun. We also used
food coloring to make red and green ones.

—Ann Riedel

Every Christmas my family would assemble a puzzle
together during the holidays. It didn't have to be a
Christmas theme—just something fun my family
picked out together. We started off with simple little
children puzzles, but as I grew, the puzzles became
more and more difficult. Once the puzzle was com-
pleted we glued it onto a piece of poster board and
we all signed and dated it with great ceremony. They
are very heart-warming to look back on as you grow.

—Kim Goehle

We started this tradition with our goddaughter and
last year were blessed to be able to include our new
son. Each Christmas Eve, before bed, we leave milk
and cookies for Santa and carrots for the reindeer

under the tree. We then read, "The Night Before Christmas" and let the kids open one gift which is always a dated ornament and hang it on the tree. When they get married, I will give each child all the ornaments they've hung over the years to share with their own families. I get teary just thinking of it.

—Janis

During the time of Advent (before Christmas) we would have the nativity scene set out. Every evening we would take turns moving Mary and Joseph around the living room, always moving a little closer to the manger on the far side of the room, symbolizing their long journey to Jerusalem. It helped us understand what Christmas was really all about.

On Christmas Eve, Mary and Joseph would finally make it safely to the manger. We would go to bed then, but St. Nicholas would actually come in the middle of the night and wake us up. Every year my dad would have a friend dress up. We would all congregate, in our pajamas and half asleep, in the living room where we would notice that the figurine of Baby Jesus had finally appeared in His little bed in the nativity scene—and St. Nicholas would talk about Christmas with us. He would then give us each a little treat and send us back to bed so he could put the rest of the presents under the tree for morning.

—Mary Belton

Every year on October 1 my three children, husband and I go to downtown Melbourne and purchase one Christmas decoration for the tree to be added to the many others we have collected along the way. My eldest son is now 20 and still waits to go on our shopping trip. We have always collected glass ornaments and have some beautiful memories recalling the year and the experience we shared on the way to the city. We always chose a different restaurant for our lunch so our decorations are also remembered by what and where we ate, and the stories those decorations brought us in previous years. Then we go home with our orna- ment, feeing that we are now "officially ready" for the festive season.

—Anne

When we were little, a good Christmas tree cost about five dollars—much more than my parents could afford—so Dad always bought our trees for

> *Don't worry about the size of your Christmas tree.*
> *In the eyes of your children they are all 30 feet tall.*
> —Larry Wilde

99 cents at Chubby & Tubby. The trees were pretty pathetic, but here's how my father turned that into a wonderful lesson and memory.

One Christmas, Dad sat us down and told us the story of, "The Little Christmas Tree That No One Wanted." As you might guess, this little tree was so homely that all the other families passed it by. As Christmas Eve approached, the homely tree huddled in the corner of the lot, stretching his little arms as wide as possible in hopes that some nice family might come by and think he was beautiful. Of course the tree was so grateful when we became that family!

One year, my father had to perform an operation on one of our Christmas trees—a "limb-andectomy." He actually cut off some branches from the bottom of the tree and then carefully "sutured" them with wire into the gaping holes at the top of the tree. It worked! Our little tree was so much prouder after my Dad's cosmetic surgery. Today, my children and I still pick the homeliest tree on the lot. We usually pay a little less for a homely tree, but we receive so much more!

—Jan Lundquist

Celebrate
the joy that kids
are always giving.
Make every day
a holiday,
and celebrate
just living.

—Betty Osborne

I started an Easter tradition with my daughter. I'll hide lots of plastic eggs around the yard (if it's nice) or inside the house. Each egg holds a little note from the Easter Bunny praising her for different accomplishments or saying things like, "You are such a good helper" or "You are a great reader!" She loves reading all the praise and she'll always write the Easter Bunny a thank you note with a little drawing. Of course, I save each one, and plan to give them to her when she's all grown up.

—Selina Sanders

When you're scattering your Easter candy for your children, stick a little piece of cotton in the door. When the kids wake up, they may think the Easter Bunny got his little tail stuck in the door on the way out.

—Emma Brodie

At Easter every year, we all became "Detective Bunny." My Dad would hide the Easter baskets around the house, and we were given clues to find them. Every clue led to a new clue and finally led to the Easter basket.

—Chelsea Pimm

What things we have seen. . .
—Francis Beumont

Before my daughter, Courtney, was old enough to really search for what the Easter Bunny had brought her, the Easter Bunny would leave a trail of cotton balls from his tail throughout the house showing where he had been. My daughter was so excited to follow the cotton balls, always finding an Easter basket of goodies at the end of the trail.
—Kim Crum

One Valentine's Day, when my son Nathan was 3, I filled his room with red and white heart balloons, with long streamers trailing from the balloons, while he was fast asleep. I videotaped his reaction when he awoke to the sea of balloons and streamers in his room. He was so delighted—he danced around his room in amazement. He is now 6 and still talks about the day the "Valentine Fairy" visited him and surprised him with so many balloons!
—Jacqueline Tarry

Valentine's Day was a really fun occasion at our house. We would usually wake up with a corny note on our pillow. It might be a picture of a rabbit with a note that said, "Some bunny loves you." A typical breakfast was heart-shaped pancakes or waffles, made with a cookie cutter. Lunch was heart-shaped sandwiches and heart-shaped cook-

*Resolved, that I will take each precious minute,
and relish all the joy within it.*
—Kathleen Rice

ies; dinner was a heart-shaped pizza, along with soup with little macaroni hearts, and Hershey's Kisses for dessert. Mom and Dad's message was always very clear: "Our love for you is everywhere."
—D.J. Haines

One of my favorite memories with my daughter is when she lost her first tooth. She was 5 years old and we put her tooth under her pillow and said good night. The Tooth Fairy came and left green fairy dust (sparkles) from the door all the way to her pillow. She was thrilled. She then proceeded to gather the dust into a small container and take it to kindergarten for show and tell. Soon the other parents complained to me because their children had come home asking why Marissa's Tooth Fairy left fairy dust, and theirs didn't!
—Tracey Lucas

When our daughter Samantha was born, my husband and I purchased a real star, including a constellation map that shows how to find it at night. There's a company on television that has been selling stars and maps for years. You get to name the star you purchase, and the company records that name so that no one else can purchase or name that particular one. When

> Love is always in the mood
> for believing in miracles.
> —John Powys

Samantha lost her first tooth, the Tooth Fairy took the tooth and placed it in the sky. Now her tooth is a golden star, and the Tooth Fairy was thoughtful enough to leave a map for her to find it at night. It is so special.
— Desley Bissett

It's easy to sprinkle a little enchantment into your Santa Claus, Easter Bunny, and Tooth Fairy. For Santa, I spread talcum powder on the floor of the children's rooms and up the hall, then donned a pair of my husband's shoes and made big footprints. For the Easter Bunny I did the same, but I made finger marks in the powder to resemble paws. For the Tooth Fairy I simply sprinkled glitter on the Venetian blinds and on the carpet near their beds. The look on their faces when they discovered these little displays was pure magic, and I have lots of snapshots to remember them by. My kids have all grown into well-balanced adults with families of their own and they too are repeating the magic of it all.
— Pamela Wyber

A truly rich man is one whose children run into his arms when his hands are empty.

—Pilar Coolinta

I have four brothers and sisters, all grown. My dad, who is still with us, gave us all a wonderful St. Patrick's Day memory when we were growing up. One by one, he took each of us on consecutive years to a grassy meadow near our home—a magic place where (he claimed) Leprechauns had frequently been sighted. It was always very early on St. Patrick's Day morning, so it was usually rainy or blustery. He always brought cinnamon rolls and hot chocolate in a thermos. Quietly (so as not to frighten the Leprechauns) we would creep to the top of a knoll and settle down with our backs against a tree to start "our watch."

For two or three hours on my chosen year—just Dad and me—we sipped hot chocolate to ward off the cold and kept our eyes peeled for the slightest movement in the long grass beneath the willows. "I thought I saw something," Dad would whisper, "over there by the post—did you see it, too?" By now, I was seeing glimpses of little green hats and boots all

*May you live in a fairy tale
where the page never turns.*
—Kobi Yamada

around me. "Do you believe?" my father would ask in a hushed tone. "Leprechauns only appear to those who believe." And, of course, by then I certainly did believe.

Then came the crowning touch! At day's end, we would wander along the edge of the meadow, looking in the grass for one last sign of a Leprechaun burrow and—wonder of wonders—we would suddenly stumble upon real Irish pennies that someone (presumably a genuine Leprechaun) had apparently dropped in the grass the night before. Did I save those Irish pennies? Twenty years later I still wear one on a chain around my neck.
—Eric Lazarre

At Thanksgiving my family always held hands in a big circle in the living room. Then we each took turns telling all the big and little things we were especially grateful for. The list grew longer and longer every year.
—Paul Dryer

Grandparents are people
with too much wisdom
to let that stop them
from making fools of
themselves over their
grandchildren.

—Phil Moss

Grandpa Fred kept a huge dark-green jar full of pennies, nickels and a few dimes on the kitchen table. Whenever we would go to Grandpa's house to help out, he would end the day by giving each of us a big cold glass of lemonade and a "dip" in the jar. You could grab as much as your hand would hold, which wasn't much. But we all knew that Grandpa was poor, so it meant a lot to him and to us. As the years rolled on, Grandpa started adding foreign coins from different countries—China, Ireland, Italy, Germany. I suppose he bought them for a couple dollars at the coin store—but what a thrill to find a genuine African coin with a zebra or an elephant on it. Years later I still have those exotic coins from Grandpa's "dip jar." They are among my most treasured possessions.

—Pat Pescatore

Much to his grandchildren's delight and amazement, my Dad grew and harvested some of the world's finest rock candy right in his own backyard. To hear Dad tell it, the cultivation of fine rock candy was a lost art that required perfect growing conditions (soil, sunlight, constant weeding, careful watering, etc.) and, of course, the steady hand of a master rock candy gardener. It was so touching to watch the children follow him out to the "rock garden," their eyes as big as saucers. The routine was always the same. Grandpa would watch sternly as the children picked up "regular" rocks and gingerly tested them with their teeth. "That one's not ripe yet," Grandpa would caution, and the children would keep searching for some that were. Finally, the master gardener himself would usher the children to a different part of the garden—someplace where the sunlight was perhaps a bit more conducive to growth—and, of course, there would always be a ripe batch of delicious rock candy at that very spot. Pure magic.

—Beth Keane

I have my children make their own greeting cards for special occasions. They personalize them, and it is much more special than buying a card from the store. P.S. Their loving Grammie saves them all!

—Melissa Robinson

Our granddaughter lives in Dallas and comes to see us for three weeks in the summer. She is 4 this year. My husband and I try to make special memories for her while she is here. Her favorite thing is to go to the Goodwill and look at the

Recall as often as you wish;
a happy memory never wears out.
—Libbie Fudim

books. She helps me dust the house so she can earn money to buy some books. Her mother wanted to take her to the Goodwill recently and my granddaughter said, "No, that's just for me and my Nana." Her Papa is building her a playhouse this year complete with front porch and windows. We hope that when she grows up she will remember the good times with Nana and Papa. I talked to her yesterday, and she can't wait to get here and we can't wait to see her.

—Bobbie Snoddy

I recently turned 80, have three grandkids, and love them all to pieces. I was born and raised in Waco, Texas, where barbecue is king. Ever since my grandson could walk and talk, he and I have been making batches of my spicy barbecue sauce. We named it, "Grandpa's Secret Sauce," and we put labels on the jars to that effect. We have been doing this for thirteen years straight, and my two granddaughters have joined in too. It's a lot of fun because when my own kids were growing up, I refused to tell them the recipe. My grandkids think it's comical that they get to know the recipe and their parents don't. I have sworn all the grandkids to secrecy, and no matter how much we get bad-gered by their parents, we just smile and shake our

*May you live long enough
to be a problem to your kids!*
—Irish Toast

heads. I have told the grandkids that they must carry on the tradition when I'm gone, and that I'll be watching from heaven just to be sure they don't get weak and spill the beans to their parents. Ha!

— Bernie Sanders

Every year my mom takes the three grandkids to her house for the week before Christmas. She has them make a list of people they would like to buy presents for, up to five. Then she takes them out to shop. It creates not just memories of shopping, but memories of spending time with Grandma and their cousins. They build snowmen and make cookies. The bonus for my sister and me is that we have time to do last minute shopping and wrap the presents, without worrying about the kids catching us.

— Tammy Moody

In the course of a child's life, pet names become a way of expressing how unique and special he or she is. Something as simple as a mispronounced name by a younger brother or sister can "stick"

115

and lead from that day forward to beautiful flashbacks of love and acceptance. "Bub" instantly takes me back to when my father held me in his arms as a small child. I hope our family's pet names will bring the same kind of joy and memories to my children and grandchildren as they get older. The simple things are the ones that remain.

—Adrienne "Bub" Eden

When our children receive a stuffed animal or doll as a gift, they name it after the person who gave it to them. For example, the latest teddy bear might be Grandma Marge, the latest rag doll Papa Ivan, etc. It's great fun having the names of our relatives on the tips of the children's tongues all the time—and, of course, they never forget the thoughtful person who gave them that gift.

—Amy Wray

My mother-in-law passed away right before I got pregnant with my daughter. She was a very special person. We want our little girl to feel like she knows her grandmother, so we keep a small

Your heart has brought great joy to many.
Those hearts can never forget you.
—Flavia Weeden

picture on her nightstand, and we tell stories about
"Bubie Leah" before she goes to bed.
—Amanda Grant Smith

Since our daughter was born (she is 3 now), my
husband and I have told her that we love her "as
big as the sky and with all my heart." My father-in-
law used to tell all the grandchildren that as he
bounced them on his knee, but he passed away
before Katie was born. I cannot express how I felt
one night when, as I tucked her in, she smiled up at
me and said, "Mommy, love you big sky and all
heart." That little saying will always be special to
her father and me, as it was to her grandfather, and
maybe one day she will be blessed with a child and
pass it on.
—Mary Haydel

I was blessed with a remarkable mother who
raised four children, including two very competitive
daughters. When it came time to divide up a
special treat (the last piece of cake, a shared candy
bar, etc.), her simple rule was: "One divides, the
other gets first choice." I've captured much of her
parenting wisdom, so I can keep passing it on in
her memory.
—Cheryl Feight

Grandparents do the strangest things sometimes, but kids love them for it. For years my Dad
took our kids to minor league baseball games in a
nearby town. Driving down to the park...arriving
early for "bat day" or "hat day"...eating peanuts,
hotdogs and Cracker Jacks...singing "Take Me Out
to the Ballgame"—these are moments my kids will
never forget.

And one more thing: Over the years Grandpa
became known at our ballpark as "the guy who
congratulates the umpire." One afternoon the
crowd started heckling the umpire over a bad call.
Our kids felt so bad for the ump that they actually
started crying. From that day forward, and
throughout every game, Grandpa made a point of
yelling out, "Nice call, ump...very perceptive...
you're doing fine, ump...keep it up!" I know it
irritated some of the fans, but my kids loved it.

About a year after my dad passed away, we got the
nicest letter from the Umpires' Association, telling
us how much they appreciated hearing Dad's voice
in the stands all those years, and how much he
would be missed. I made copies of that letter and
had them framed for all the grandkids.

—Carl Brodeur

Time prevails but cannot fade the memories that love has made.
—Norma Howland

I conceived my daughter two weeks after my father-in-law passed away. And while Katie has never met her grandfather, we have shown her lots of pictures and told her a lot about him, including that he sometimes drove a crane. Now whenever she sees a crane, she says, "Look, its Papa's crane." Even though he is not here with us, he is still a memorable part of my daughter's life and hopefully she will grow up knowing that even though he is in heaven, he will remain a big part of her life.
— Mary Haydel

Grandma Helen had a wonderful ritual she did with all her grandchildren. It was such a simple thing, but it made us feel special. Whenever she baked pies, or cakes, or even tuna casseroles, she would always make miniature ones for the kids. Your very own miniature apple pie—what a special treat!
— Fred Dwyer

Mom and Dad
had a thousand
wonderful ways to
say, "We love you,"
without ever actually
saying it at all.

—Jerome Riggs

What comes from the heart goes to the heart.
—Samuel Taylor Coleridge

Ever since I was a little girl my dad and I had a secret code to communicate how much we loved each other. While holding hands our special message went like this: He would squeeze four times, which meant, "Do you love me?" I would squeeze three times, replying, "Yes I do." He would squeeze two times asking, "How much?" Then I would respond by squeezing as hard as I could to indicate how much I loved him. I can't wait until my 9-month-old son, Alex, is old enough to play the "I love you" game with me.

— Michelle Bunje

When my toddler had separation anxiety, I would put on lipstick and give her a kiss on her hand. Anytime she missed me, she'd just look down and see the lipstick kiss on her hand and feel better. Today she's 9 years old and still remembers!

— Mary G. Jones

Even before children can talk, they can learn to sign. We taught our little son to sign, "I love you." Now whenever we put him to bed, or leave him with the babysitter or at Grandma's, we always sign our love to each other.

— Kelly Birch

Find something in every day
that makes your heart smile.
—Kobi Yamada

About the second week after my daughter was born I decided it was very important that we both start the day off with lots of love and smiles and music. I came up with a tune and made a song with the letters of her name. It goes like this: "I" is for INCREDIBLE. "S" is for SMILEY. "A" is for ADORABLE. "B" is for BEAUTIFUL. "E" is for ELECTRIFYING. "L" is for LOVING. "L" is for LOVED. And "A" is for AMAZING. Put them all together and they spell ISABELLA, ISABELLA, ISABELLA BABY! That is the song she hears every single morning. Even my husband wakes up and  says, "Are you going to sing the song now?" Singing this song to her every morning fills me with a warm spirit, brings a smile to both of us, and deepens the love and connection I have with my daughter every day. Sometimes when she is cranky at midday I will start singing the song, and she will immediately turn to smiles! My hope is that when she is older she will remember that

Where love is present, life is always full.
—Gerome Guiles

every day is positive and filled with love. When we have our second child, maybe Isabella will be able to help me create a song for her brother or sister.
—Yaffa Carlson

Whenever I want to kiss my 3-year-old son, Jake, I always request to kiss somewhere different. "May I kiss your elbow? Your knee? Your ear-lobe?" It always makes him giggle no matter what kind of mood he's in.
—Beth Seabreeze

Every day I say to my two girls, "Who loves you?" And they answer, "Mummy does." Then I say, " Who is beautiful?" And they say, "Allana and Hayley." Then I say, "Who is clever?" And they answer, "Allana and Hayley." This little ritual helps them realize that they are beautiful girls and can do anything they want to do—always with the love and support of their mom.
—Amanda Smith

Our daughter will celebrate her first birthday soon. We started our "group hug" when she was just an infant. We'd hold her, and then my husband and I would wrap our arms around each other for a mini group hug. She now looks forward to it

Kind words of appreciation will sing in their memory for years.
—Brenda Richards

several times a day, especially in the morning before we go to work and in the evening when we return home to each other. We want this memory to mean that, "No matter how hard the day, our group hugs give us energy and keep us connected as a family."
—Kelly Layman

As a new mother, I brainstormed on traditions that I would love to start with my new daughter. I have come up with so many but my favorite and most simple advice is to say something beautiful and sweet to your little one every day. It won't take but a minute and it will last in their minds forever. I tell my daughter every day that I think she's beautiful, and I am so proud to have her as my daughter.
—Debra Rajpatee

Every night before going to bed, my 2-year-old son, Ruger, and I sing a song we call, "Who Loves Ruger?" I start off by singing, "Mama loves you Ruger!" Then I allow him to choose the next person and we sing it together. He names all the people in his life that he knows love him. From "Dada loves you Ruger!" to "Grandma loves you Ruger!" He calls out cousins' names, his babysitter, aunts and uncles, even family pets. It's a special way to end the day, and it helps Ruger realize how much he is loved by many people, and how important he is to us all.

—Lisa Robles

Write a poem to each of your children. Call it, "What I Love About (your child's name)." I have done this for each of my kids and put it in their baby books. I know they will cherish it one day. Do things you wish your parents would have done for you. You may not be around to tell your children later in life the little things they may want to know. For example, "I love the way my daughter thinks anything with four wheels is called a car."

—Tammeye Crawford

When my son was just a toddler we developed a special "love language." Anytime we wanted to say, "I love you," but didn't want to say it out loud, we would blink real hard to each other. This worked at the dinner table as well as when he was across the room. As he grew, it became encouragement—whether he was singing carols at the front of the church as a pre-schooler or looking for reassurance to get through a third-grade play.

Now my son is 13 and it is not "cool" for a mother to say "I love you" as she drops him off for school. But our "love blinks" get us through. He can secretly accept them, smiling and without embarrassment.

Of course, "love blinks" work both ways. I have been diagnosed with lupus and on days that I need extra strength to get through, I look up into my doorway and see my son standing there looking so tall, so "teen-age," and he is giving me "love blinks" making me smile and easing my pain. I once asked him what he thought about my sharing our "love blinks" idea with others and he said, "That's cool, everyone needs a blink once in a while!"

—Sheila Essen

May life's
greatest gifts
always be yours—

happiness, memories,
and dreams.

—Josie Bissett

Send us your Parenting Tips and Memory Makers!

We are currently planning new editions of
Making Memories and *Little Bits of Wisdom*
and invite you to contribute yours.
Just visit our website today.
Thank you for your contribution:
www.littlebitsofwisdom.com

To order additional copies of
Making Memories or *Little Bits of Wisdom*,
or other inspiring Compendium products,
call or write today:

COM·PEN′·DI·UM™
Publishing

Enriching the lives of millions, one person at a time.

This book may be ordered directly from the
publisher, but please try your local bookstore first!

Call toll free (800) 91-IDEAS

6325 212th St. SW, Suite K,
Lynnwood, WA 98036

www.compendiuminc.com